Fearsome Rhymes

Edited By Catherine Cook

First published in Great Britain in 2019 by:

Young Writers
Remus House
Coltsfoot Drive
Peterborough
PE2 9BF
Telephone: 01733 890066
Website: www.youngwriters.co.uk

All Rights Reserved
Book Design by Ashley Janson
© Copyright Contributors 2019
Softback ISBN 978-1-83928-589-9

Printed and bound in the UK by BookPrintingUK
Website: www.bookprintinguk.com
YB0426N

FOREWORD

Hello Reader!

For our latest poetry competition we sent out funky and vibrant worksheets for primary school pupils to fill in and create their very own poem about fiendish fiends and crazy creatures. I got to read them and guess what? They were **roarsome**!

The pupils were able to read our example poems and use the fun-filled free resources to help bring their imaginations to life, and the result is pages **oozing** with exciting poetic tales. From friendly monsters to mean monsters, from bumps in the night to **rip-roaring** adventures, these pupils have excelled themselves, and now have the joy of seeing their work in print!

Here at Young Writers we love nothing more than poetry and creativity. We aim to encourage children to put pen to paper to inspire a love of the written word and explore their own unique worlds of creativity. We'd like to congratulate all of the aspiring authors that have created this book of **monstrous mayhem** and we know that these poems will be enjoyed for years to come. So, dive on in and submerge yourself in all things furry and fearsome (and perhaps check under the bed!).

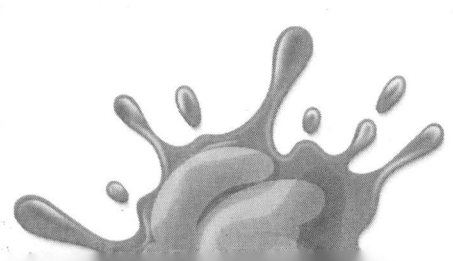
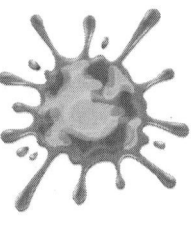

CONTENTS

Acorns Primary School, Preston

Jacob Jones (8)	1
Samuel Lunn (8) & Luke Butler	2
Bethany Laverty (10)	3

Blacklands Primary School, Kilwinning

Ella Torrance (9)	4
Harris Napier (10)	5
Chloe Bryden (10)	6
Millie Porter (9)	7
Chelsea Rose Rocks (10)	8
Kayla Wilson (8)	9
Skye Little (10)	10

Blackwell Primary School, Blackwell

Lewis Cutts (8)	11

Blenheim Road Community Primary School, St Dials

Freya Neagle-Ceretti (11)	12
Honey Thacker (10)	14
Aerona Hughes (10)	15

Caistor CE & Methodist Primary School, Caistor

Jack Wells (10)	16

Howardian Primary School, Cardiff

Maddie Thompson (9)	18
Alisha Ali (7)	20
Seren de Mendonca (7)	21
Lounis Blanc-Menad (8)	22
Beth Davies-Seed (9)	23
Anisa Islam (9)	24
Ava Longomo (7)	25
Amelia Dunscombe (8)	26
Freyja Aria Jones (8)	27
Amelia Davison Crean (8)	28
Sophia Case (7)	29
Hala Mohammad Alasadii (7)	30
Scarlett Reid (8)	31
Alisha Ashraf (9)	32
Aleeza Ali (8)	33
Dylan Cross (8)	34
Malakai Carter (7)	35
Chloe Griffiths (8)	36
Venus Wu (8)	37
Lanna Khorshid (8)	38
Tilly-Rose Stanworth (8)	39
Caden Jay Bridle (8)	40
Kamile Skwarczynska (8)	41
Sofia Salter (8)	42
Charlotte Abric (8)	43
Asmaa Babiker Mohammed (7)	44
Rhys Karseras (7)	45
Felix Pateman (7)	46
Lamar Sami Mohamed (7)	47
Joshua Ashley (7)	48
Evie Louise Fish (7)	49
Isabelle Pembroke (7)	50
Leo William Outten (7)	51

Ashton Burt (7)	52
Omar Sami Mohamed (8)	53
Dexter Howl Cadby (7)	54
Grace Delve (7)	55
Harry Allan (8)	56
Rahma Mustafa Al-Qaysi (8)	57
Lola Gent (8)	58
Nia Owen (8)	59
Charley Davis Vickers (8)	60
Nye Brute-Woods (8)	61
Eira Wolski (7)	62
Llywelyn Lewis (7)	63
Mariam Amin (7)	64
Titi Oladebo (8)	65
Raya Shemshaki (8)	66
Harlen Rochford Taylor (7)	67
Rosie Thomas (7)	68
Ben Davies (8)	69
Jada Johannes (7)	70
Lewis Walker (7)	71
Rai Pequito (8)	72
Amaani Majid (7)	73
Amelia Sadiq (8)	74
Mohamad Almezyab (8)	75
Samuel Parsons (8)	76
Angus Turton (7)	77
Alby Atherton (7)	78
Flora Szabo (7)	79
Samuel Giles (7)	80
Zachary William Ait-Hammi (8)	81
Bob McCarthy (8)	82
Macy Thomas (8)	83
Olly Williams (7)	84
Akshara Madahar (8)	85
Daniyal Ali (9)	86
Zachary Weston (8)	87
Maja Fogarty (8)	88
Louie Philip Smith (8)	89
Caia Chiu (7)	90
Abdul-Wahhab Amin (8)	91
Siyam Ali (7)	92
Elliot Hoyt (7)	93
Aleix Pacheco (8)	94

Evan Rhys Andrews (7)	95
Jacob William Harrison (7)	96
Elizabeth Stocks (7)	97
Berguzar Masal Yalcin (7)	98
Mia Cuddihy (7)	99
Adam Zaczynski (7)	100
Aeron William Cording (8)	101
Christine Zhang (7)	102
Jackson Turner (7)	103

Millway Primary School, Duston

Naomi Pinto (8)	104
Eloise Baker (8)	105
Olivia Saunders (8)	106
Edmund Puchovic (8)	107
Peaches Gooding (8)	108

Real Action Butterfly School, Queens Park

Amir (10)	109

Sacred Heart Primary School, Battersea

Anujan Rejonald Nirubaraj (8)	110

Sneinton CE Primary School, Sneinton

Anagha Vinod Nair (9)	111
Ivie Daniella Enoma (8)	112

Sowerby Village CE (VC) Primary School, Sowerby Bridge

Ebony Setter (6)	113
James William Speight (6)	114
JJ Riley (6)	115
Zachary Pukl (6)	116
Ryan Martin Lynch (6)	117
Libby Lewis (7)	118
Amelia Pollard (6)	119
Milli-Sue Graham (6)	120

St Mark's CE (VA) Primary School, Talbot Village

Evie Williams (7)	121
Ryan Hegan (9)	122
Emma Gheorghe (9)	124
Lexi Mae Shakespeare (8)	126
Sa'ad Rehan Sami (8)	127
Josie Aston (7)	128
Christopher Ngwenya Pickering (8)	129
Elsy Beales (9)	130
Jayden You (7)	131
Felicity Tschoepe (8)	132
Mirabella Twardowska (7)	133
Josh Horgan (9)	134
Ava-Louise Parris (7)	135
Annabel Hitchins (8)	136
Sam Treliving (7)	137
Tasmin Addis (9)	138
Louis Paull (7)	139
Zara Guppy (9)	140
Summer-Bella Hack (7)	141
George William Lowton (7)	142
Josh Jabulani Nyathi (7)	143
Layla Kwok (7)	144

The Compass Primary Academy, Kettering

Darcy Joseph Fletcher (8)	145
Bethany Hull (8)	146
Maria Ignat (9)	147
Sanjeda Ahmed (8)	148
Harrison Bridgman (9)	149
Harmonaii Lily Jean Wood (8)	150
Wiktor Kopania (8)	151
Aiden Knell (8)	152
Thomas Pickford (8)	153
Zara Treadwell (8)	154
Jaidan Webb (7)	155
Zack Lewis Whiteman (8)	156
Maisie Bell (7)	157
Devon Cook (8)	158

Cameron Rhys Wonfor (8)	159
Abby Chamberlain (8)	160
Faith Lillie Elrick (7)	161
Ashley Ridley (10)	162
Yaw Boateng Amoakohene (8)	163
Emily Collett (8)	164
Maisey Angela Horrigan (7)	165
Dexter Whitney-Green (7)	166
Harley Chiam (9)	167
Scarlett Rayner (9)	168
Violet Serendipity Haywood (9)	169
Kaja Kajszczarek (7)	170
Ivo Otocki (7)	171
Ellie-Louise Frost (9)	172
Thomas Angusdon Rogers (7)	173
Isabella Cross (8)	174
Hollie-Beth Howlin (7)	175
Carmelo Chowanski (9)	176
Reese Stapleford (9)	177
Archie Roe (7)	178
Blake Sidney Robert Smith-Edwards (7)	179
Harri Taylor (9)	180

Ysgol Pum Heol, Llanelli

Michael Wetton (10)	181
Cadi Fflur Desouza (10)	182

THE POEMS

Dino Monster

D angerous teeth, just like Holly.
I feel scared.
N o, I don't want to be eaten.
O h no!

Jacob Jones (8)
Acorns Primary School, Preston

Dino Monster

D angerous teeth,
I feel scared.
N o, I don't want to be eaten!
O h no!

Samuel Lunn (8) & Luke Butler
Acorns Primary School, Preston

Dino Monster

D angerous jaws,
I t has claws,
N ot nice!
O h no!

Bethany Laverty (10)
Acorns Primary School, Preston

Poppy

Stinky Poppy is a little girl
With a big secret under her sleeves.
The light hurts humans about 100 times
But she loves the moon and stars because they come out.

In the day, in the day she is Poppy
But at night she is stinky Poopy.
Now she is a monster, she only likes crunchy and juicy food.
Okay, now you know her, let me tell you something...
You're next!

Ella Torrance (9)
Blacklands Primary School, Kilwinning

Randy The Rubbish Monster

Beware when you put your rubbish in the bin,
Randy the Rubbish Monster lives there like a king.
Randy will be lurking, watching your every move.
He will be sorting through your rubbish
Until you need to move.
He is always hungry, never full,
Every bit of rubbish makes him drool.
He is very annoying, also very cruel,
So remember to watch out for Randy.

Harris Napier (10)
Blacklands Primary School, Kilwinning

Meany Mence

M ichael and
E astern
A te
N inety-thousand humans
"Y ummy," said both of them.

"M ore, more!" screamed Michael
E astern ran for the kids,
"N o one will be left, mwahaha!"
C urtis came along, "No, not me!"
E veryone was dead.

Chloe Bryden (10)
Blacklands Primary School, Kilwinning

Cute Monster Holly In The Bin

Be careful when you go
To put your rubbish in the bin.
Holly the monster lives in it but it's okay
Because she is very funny and kind.
She will come out of the bin sometimes, probably.
Her favourite food is mince and potatoes,
Yummy in my tummy!
You know I like it myself too, it is very good.

Millie Porter (9)
Blacklands Primary School, Kilwinning

Zoe's Birthday

M onster Zoe was in her bed
O n Monday, it was her birthday
N one would forget her birthday
S unday passed, her birthday, was today
T he TV was on but there was no one
E veryone forgot her birthday but everyone bought her a
R ange Rover for her birthday.

Chelsea Rose Rocks (10)
Blacklands Primary School, Kilwinning

Tim The Tickle Monster

Hi, my name is Tim the Tickle Monster.
I tickle everyone I see,
I will tickle your feet when you're asleep.
Make you cry with laughter
And forget the fright.
Boo!

Kayla Wilson (8)
Blacklands Primary School, Kilwinning

Puffy Boo

P retty, playful and cute
U nique and chubby
F at and on fleek
F unny and puffy.

Skye Little (10)
Blacklands Primary School, Kilwinning

Blue

My monster's name is Blue
He really likes to roar
He lives in a dark, blue cave
And when he sleeps, he snores!

His breath smells like rotten cabbages
It's bright blue like you've never seen
It mixes with the sensational, blazing yellow sun
And turns his breath bright green

Roooaaaarrr!

Lewis Cutts (8)
Blackwell Primary School, Blackwell

Mr Alive

Mr Alive can give a big roar,
Mr Alive is an adventurous monster.
Adventurous Aaronel is his monstrous name,
His fur is as solid as a still hard rock.
His eyebrows are as fluffy as a Pomeranian,
His sharp teeth are full of the blood of the night-time.
Be careful, Aaronel! Don't touch the light!
He has a bony crack in the middle,
I don't know why,
But that monster really needs a chill pill!
If you wanted to go near him, he would cut out your limb,
Aaronel loved Hell school, but hated his teacher, Mrs Love,
She was so lovely, all the boys stared
While walking down the corridor with her.
Of course, Aaronel hated love,
But other than that, he really liked bats.
Mr Alive is the secondary king,

If you went near him, he would fling!
Mr Alive is my pet
No need to fear him, you'll just get him upset!

Freya Neagle-Ceretti (11)
Blenheim Road Community Primary School, St Dials

Spiky Mikey

I saw him in the middle of the night,
Spiky Mikey gave me a fright,
Moving left, moving right,
I held my breath as he moved through the night,
His whole body covered in spikes like a hedgehog,
I struggled to see him through the dark and the fog,
I caught his eye, so scary and red,
I began to panic and thought I was dead,
We stared at each other for a moment or two,
I instantly knew I needed the loo,
Spiky Mikey turned and ran away,
I will never forget that scary day!

Honey Thacker (10)
Blenheim Road Community Primary School, St Dials

Love Monsters

Love Monster loves us all,
It doesn't matter if you're small or tall,
He'll love you every day.

If you're young or old,
I've been told
He may send a kiss your way!

If it's just a hug you need,
He'll do a good deed
And 'I love you' is all he'll say.

Aerona Hughes (10)
Blenheim Road Community Primary School, St Dials

My Friend, Tim!

Lying in my bed,
Listening, waiting,
Creaking floorboards echo through the silent halls,
Scratching my nails on the walls.

Nowhere to run, nowhere to hide,
As the big clock strikes ten,
The door opens wide.

A strong stench fills the air,
Gripping my sheets as they tear,
Shocking, shivering, wondering who's there,
As I reach for my flashlight,
As I prepare for a fright in the spooky, dark night.

The sheet gets pulled from over my head,
I see a monster-like creature at the foot of my bed,
One big eye was staring at me wide,
Making me want to run and hide,
Standing three feet tall with a big cheesy grin,
His squeaky voice says, "Hi! My name's Tim!"

He spreads out his wings, jumping around with joy,
"Please will you be my friend, little boy?"

From now on when the lights are dim,
He comes out to play,
He's my monster friend Tim!

Jack Wells (10)
Caistor CE & Methodist Primary School, Caistor

The Slimy, Silly Monster And The Little Girl

Mr Slimy Silly Monster's eyes are as white as clouds
His voice is very loud...
He won't let me sleep.
He always comes out and peeps!
He has the face of an old lady.
He has a small head but bumpy like a baby.
He always hides and crouches.
He always smells and carries pouches.
He looks like a bear.
He also opens the door.
Then he flies up so high,
Up, up, up into the sky.
He looks so blue
He wears two pairs of shoes.
It's so bright and so so light
It smells like underwear,
That's been over there.
I don't like Smelly Monsters but I like this one

Oh no, it's run away!
Please come back, another day!

Maddie Thompson (9)
Howardian Primary School, Cardiff

The Three-Eyed Monster

Tonight is very spooky,
So spooky you will be scared.
But the three-eyed monster is there for you,
So be prepared.
All the horror movies are all so spooky,
So instead of popcorn, you can have a cookie.
Now, I know it's not as spooky as last year
But this autumn, it's the three-eyed monster that you'll hear.
Nightmares, horror movies and all of that stuff
All rolled into a very little ball of some comfortable, fluffy and hairy fluff.
As soon as you listen to this rhyme,
It will make you think about the jungle vines.
This poem is very true
And it'll make you feel very, very light blue.
All the nightmares are rolled into one.

Alisha Ali (7)
Howardian Primary School, Cardiff

The Superstar

Hair longer than Rapunzel
And horns longer than a unicorn's.
Dressed posher than a castle.
Skin greener than green slime
And make-up prettier than a human pop star.
Eyes brighter than the big, hot sun
And a nose waxier than earwax.
Its lips are redder than lipstick.
Teeth are sharper than a shark.
Shoes prettier than violet rock.
Its song is better than a human's life voice.
The moon is lighter than a sunset
And the grass is darker than the night.
Its earrings are violet coloured and nicer than gold.
Its hands are as orange as Doritos.
Its party hat is as beautiful as a diamond.

Seren de Mendonca (7)
Howardian Primary School, Cardiff

Inside The Dark Mountain Cave

One night with no light, in a dark mountain cave.
I was looking for some glimmering, shimmering diamonds.
Suddenly I saw something move!
I was so so nervous.
In the dark mountain cave, it smelt horrendous.
I saw a very jagged diamond, it was a giant purple diamond.
It transformed into a monster that was called Crusher!
I tried to run away, but with his gigantic hammerhead, he bashed the entrance.
He then turned back and stared at me.
He raised his hand up, I thought he was going to kill me, but instead, he gave me a big hug.
That is my poem of the Crusher.

Lounis Blanc-Menad (8)
Howardian Primary School, Cardiff

Under The Stinky Sewers

One drippy night...
The smell of drains was very bad
It would make my nose quite red!
I bet that those that live under there must feel quite sad!
I could hear the drips of water from the top of the drain
And I think I could hear the splatter of the rain too!
I've heard that the Slobby lives under there.
Now I bet you're wondering what the Slobby is...
Watch out, he's behind you!
Okay, false alarm, I just wanted to see your fear.
Now I'd better get some sleep
But let's hope he doesn't creep.

Beth Davies-Seed (9)
Howardian Primary School, Cardiff

A Slimy Street

One was looking around in my bed,
Listening to my mum shout in her bed.
Then I heard something in the slimy street,
Thinking that someone's friends might finally meet.
I sneak outside my house door,
Trying to hear this so-called roar.
Then I saw something spiky,
Yelling something like... "Hikey".
Then he saw me and tried to eat me,
"Ahh, wait, what's that? I think that's your mummy."
He ran away to a faraway land.
He also took some children to eat
Because he loves meat.

Anisa Islam (9)
Howardian Primary School, Cardiff

The Scary Vampire

Teeth are whiter than the clouds.
They have white, pale skin.
Hair is as dark as a black dress.
Their friendly bat is pitch-black.
They kill people.
Its teeth are sharper than a shark.
Its clothes are darker than the night sky.
The moon is whiter than a rubber.
They eat at night.
Their horn is sharper than a shark.
Its voice is scarier than Annabelle.
They're as terrifying as tarantulas,
As smelly as the dump.
Their nails are sharper than a spider.

Ava Longomo (7)
Howardian Primary School, Cardiff

A Noisy Night

I was once lying in my bed
And felt a drip upon my head.
I looked straight up and there I saw
Something I'd never seen before!
A monster clinging like stalactites,
A monster, I can tell you, it gave me quite a fright!
He couldn't hold on anymore
And came down, *splat,* on the floor!
But instead of letting out a mighty roar,
He went squirming for the door!
Alone again, I went back to sleep
And these are some memories I'm sure to keep!

Amelia Dunscombe (8)
Howardian Primary School, Cardiff

One Spooky Halloween

One spooky Halloween I heard a scream,
It was awfully loud.
I ran home and again and again
It got louder and louder.
Soon it stopped but I saw a door.
I opened the door and I saw a monster.
It was big, it was frightening,
It had big, sharp teeth,
It had no legs.
I ran and ran until I was stuck.
It dived closer and closer
It had a dark kind of power.
It touched me and I fell asleep.
I hope it goes away
So I can have a nice Halloween.

Freyja Aria Jones (8)
Howardian Primary School, Cardiff

The Fluffy Night

At midnight he strikes with his big, fluffy pipe.
He has hairy little feet on his big, long legs.
On my toes, I can feel his fluffy wheel.
He has horns on his head, that's why he's Fred.
He stinks of cheese and he's not good to greet.
Under my warm bed, I smell Fred.
I can smell his feet in my bed
I can feel his short little head.
He is very small for a Fred.
In my mouth, I'm about to be sick
Because I'm smelling this cheesy mix.

Amelia Davison Crean (8)
Howardian Primary School, Cardiff

The Story Of Pretty Precious Pamela

Teeth are as sharp as glass.
Eyes as fiery as lava.
Wings as beautiful as wedding dresses.
Slime as slimy as slugs.
Whoosh! goes the monster.
Crash! goes the monster.
Roar!
It sucks blood like vampires but scarier.
Legs as fast as a cheetah.
It wakes in the night and scares children.
Argh, what is that?
It goes into a cave and scares little bats.
Scwee! Scwee! What is that?

Sophia Case (7)
Howardian Primary School, Cardiff

Hat-Wearing Hala Monster

They crawl under the children's bed,
It was a windy and scary night
And the children were terrifying.
The monsters were stomping like a dinosaur
And the monster was a hat.
His teeth were as sharp as a knife
And he had an angry face!
His eyes were as red as fire.
His mouth was as smelly as a cheese
When the wind was whooshing,
The curtains were swinging and
The toys were flying across the ceiling!

Hala Mohammad Alasadii (7)
Howardian Primary School, Cardiff

The Blobby Fright!

One day I was playing with slime
but then something gave me such a fright.
I looked to see what I had made
but then my mum made me do what I hate.
Going to bed wasn't what I'd planned in my head,
I brought my slime monster up to bed.
In my head, I was dreaming sweet dreams
but then my slime monster turned real
and scared my eyeballs out of me...
For what I saw, was an ugly, cross-eyed monster.

Scarlett Reid (8)
Howardian Primary School, Cardiff

The Midnight Monster

Monty the Midnight Monster is a sight of fright,
Watch out, he can really bite.
He lives under your bed,
Beware, you could be dead.
Monty is always as quiet as a mouse,
He can smell like very bad poo around your house.
He can be very saucy and cheeky,
You won't like it when he's leaky.
When he's at your house there is no moon,
He doesn't like the sun, so he's not out at noon.

Alisha Ashraf (9)
Howardian Primary School, Cardiff

Spooky Night

Smelly socks through the scary, sticky swamp.
Quickly, run before the scary monster gets you, only two miles!
In the deep dark forest,
There are sounds you have heard before.
So many directions, I don't know where to go.
Catch up before the monster catches you.
Holding her breath before she spits out
As she stinks up the whole swamp.
Yay, don't say, that the monster is going to catch us, run!

Aleeza Ali (8)
Howardian Primary School, Cardiff

A Cold Night

One cold night,
I had a fright.
A slime blob fell on my hand,
It was gooey but gritty like sand.

A slimy monster stood next to my bed.
At first I was scared but then he said,
"I'm Big Blobby, I'm friendly and kind,
I'm looking for a friend but they're hard to find."

"I'll be your friend," I said.
Then we played games on my bed.

Dylan Cross (8)
Howardian Primary School, Cardiff

Monster Malakai

Eyes like a devil.
Bang! went the monster's big feet.
Teeth like a needle.
Head as big as Earth.
Legs like a wiggly worm.
Hair like a sharp knife.
Skin as stinky as rotten cheese.
Crash! Bang! went the monster's feet.
Whoosh! went the flying monster.
His teeth as sharp as steel
Feet like a bony skull.
Muscles as big as a boxer.

Malakai Carter (7)
Howardian Primary School, Cardiff

A Scary Night

One scary night, I was in bed, dozing away,
Asleep in my special bed.
Then a scary 'bang' came from below my bed,
It sounded so mushy and scary.
Then I fell off my bed like a bat!
And there was jelly on the floor,
Like a squishy floor?
Then it exploded like a volcano.
The door opened like there was a ghost.
Of course, I was scared but it never came out of my head.

Chloe Griffiths (8)
Howardian Primary School, Cardiff

A Starry Night

One night I saw loads of slime bombs, just like firebombs.
Well, he robs and pops,
Shouts and sings.
People chop just like onions.
Don't make a peep, be asleep.
When he comes, he will chuck you out.
I went downstairs to get a drink,
I think it's a monster!
I am really scared, what will he do to me?
Is he going to squirt venom at me?
What is he going to do?

Venus Wu (8)
Howardian Primary School, Cardiff

Ghost The Monster

A monster is hovering in my room.
I can smell him blowing a wall down.
Ahh, he's in my room!
It can't be true, it's Ghost the monster.
I say. "Ghost, why have you come into my room with a broom and a balloon?"
Did I mention, he likes to eat children?
When I look away he jumps away.
At last, he's away.
Now I get to go to sleep, without a peep.

Lanna Khorshid (8)
Howardian Primary School, Cardiff

Molly Munch

Molly Munch is as hungry as a monkey
That hasn't been fed for days!
She hides under the bed,
Looking for bread.
At midnight, she strikes,
Hoping the food won't be any price.
She is as cute as a cat
But she's as fierce as a bat.
Molly Munch strikes night,
She might give you quite a fright.
If you cut your hair,
She might give you a dare!

Tilly-Rose Stanworth (8)
Howardian Primary School, Cardiff

The Deadly

When I was sleeping,
Under my bed there was a monster!
"Argh!" I shouted.
I saw a phoenix monster.
I jumped out of bed,
Ran to the door
And slammed the door.
But there was a knock on the door!
So I opened the door
And he tried to bite me.
He had a sharp horn
And a stringy body with lots of scars.
Then we made friends.

Caden Jay Bridle (8)
Howardian Primary School, Cardiff

The Crazy Monster Called Fred In My Bed

I go to find a drink
And when I come back I find a monster in my bed
I name him Fred
Fred is really good at hide-and-seek
The crazy monster's favourite colour is dark blue
like a cow's moo
I can smell the rotten flour in the kitchen
I think it's the monster ghost
If he sees you and you get scared by Fred
You will turn into his friend.

Kamile Skwarczynska (8)
Howardian Primary School, Cardiff

Mighty Fright

The Mighty Fright is on the roof
So watch out so you don't get bombed.
He's coming to eat you.
He splats on the ground and it falls back to Earth.
His breath smells like chicken and ice cream,
Eww, it stinks,
So gross.
The Mighty Fright only comes at night.
Hide under your covers
I can feel slime in my bedroom dripping everywhere.

Sofia Salter (8)
Howardian Primary School, Cardiff

The Bloohey House

One night, something gave me a fright!
Something created out of slime, something lime...
I took a closer look but all I could see was his back.
I ran back to bed to see him following me!
His head was sharp as a butcher's knife.
As morning came, *poof!* He disappeared.
I hope he never comes back
Our lives will be ruined if he comes back.

Charlotte Abric (8)
Howardian Primary School, Cardiff

Amazing Asmaa

He has white, pale skin.
His teeth are whiter than clouds.
His arms are longer than an octopus
And as blue as the sea and the night sky.
His skin is darker than the night sky.
His eyes are redder than blood.
His tummy is lumpy like jelly.
His voice is scarier than Annabelle.
His nose is bumpy like rotten cheese
And looks like a volcano.

Asmaa Babiker Mohammed (7)
Howardian Primary School, Cardiff

Killer Cook's Revenge

Skin as slimy as a ship's mess.
Killer Cook swoops around the forest, dropping poisoned treats,
Smelly chocolate, green cheese and a cake with a red bush berry.
A bat flew among the trees, had a bite
And dropped through the leaves.
Whoosh! went the flying monster,
Cackling all the way.
"It's time to play! Ha ha ha."

Rhys Karseras (7)
Howardian Primary School, Cardiff

Hairy Henry's Midnight Strike

Eyes like hypnotic rings.
Breath like the moon.
Whoosh! goes the rushing wind through his fur.
Teeth are as sharp as an axe.
Claws like vampire fangs.
Fur as soft as silk.
Colours like a rainbow.
As big as a house.
Friends like a bull in a china shop.
Habitat is like the dump.
Fire in his eyes.
Food is like mud.

Felix Pateman (7)
Howardian Primary School, Cardiff

The Story Of Slimy Gloomy Monster

Bang! goes the terrifying monster with big, heavy feet.
Eyes as terrifying as a volcano erupting.
Slime as slimy as an ugly snail.
Skin warty like a witch's ugly nose.
Smelly skin, putrid like mouldy, rotten, slimy cheese.
Hair as fluffy as a puppy's fur.
Whoosh goes the windy trees,
Scaring the children as they sleep.

Lamar Sami Mohamed (7)
Howardian Primary School, Cardiff

Bloodsucking Monster

With glowing red eyes,
The bloodsucking monster comes out at night,
Scaring the sleeping children in their homes.
Ready to suck their blood,
The monster comes into a new home at ninety-six.
Ready to open the door, it opens
And he walks upstairs.
Creaking the staircase,
He climbs up the bannister...
Creak, creak, creak!

Joshua Ashley (7)
Howardian Primary School, Cardiff

Mrs Pop

Watch out! Mrs Pop is coming,
She's funny and gentle if you're being good.
But if you have sweets, she will take them,
And if you're awake, she'll give you nightmares.
She is so creepy!
If you shout, she'll give you sprouts for tea.
I'm on my bed and I see a shadow of a head,
Watch out, her tail is like a snake!

Evie Louise Fish (7)
Howardian Primary School, Cardiff

Monster Of The Dark

Be careful when you're in the dark,
Where monsters lurk and monsters lark.
My monster is a hundred feet tall,
She's bigger than a gigantic wall.
Her hair is all slimy,
All gruesome and grimy.
She swims like a fish,
In one big swish.
She's spiky and prickly too,
Be careful or she will get you!

Isabelle Pembroke (7)
Howardian Primary School, Cardiff

Mrs Fat Monster Killed The City

Watch out!
Mrs Fat Monster is coming.
Hope you hide under your bed,
Because if you don't hide anywhere,
Then you'll be caught by Mrs Fat Monster.
Luckily you're hiding under your bed
So you won't get caught by Mrs Fat Monster.
She is ginormous.
She will take away your pencil case and eat it!

Leo William Outten (7)
Howardian Primary School, Cardiff

Ashton The Monster

My monster has blue fur like the sky.
His eyeballs are as round as a pie.
At night in bed, his skin turns red.
In the morning, he's got loads of energy
After that, he is a smart scientist,
Who likes playing with chemistry.
He's always laughing and full of joy,
He goes to the park with his favourite boy.

Ashton Burt (7)
Howardian Primary School, Cardiff

A Slimy Day

Slimy Simon is as sticky as glue
And his favourite colour is sea blue.
He is as slimy as goo.
He hides under people's beds
And his favourite colour bed is lots of different reds.
He really smells like sweaty PE kits.
He is really scary when he roars.
Be careful, so he doesn't get into your drawers.

Omar Sami Mohamed (8)
Howardian Primary School, Cardiff

The Lazy Monster Story

My monster is short, hairy and fat
And he likes to rap
He eats gold chains
And it drives him insane
He is weird but kind
But always keeps you in mind
He always wears a big golden watch
So he is always on time
My monster may be hairy and weird
But he has a big heart so he isn't very scary.

Dexter Howl Cadby (7)
Howardian Primary School, Cardiff

Psychopathic Monster

I can hear him hissing under the bed.
"I will not let the cow killer kill you tonight,"
Grandma said.
He has a great artistic skill
And a license to kill, kill and kill.
He might leave you with cuts and scars
That will make you feel pain.
It will hurt so bad,
It will drive you insane.

Grace Delve (7)
Howardian Primary School, Cardiff

Destroyer Layer

His voice has a deep tone
Which sounds a bit like lava.
Also, be careful in the dark,
Otherwise, he'll kill you on the mark.
He eats you like a sandwich, *crunch, crunch!*
He goes, "Ahh, I had something to tell you straight away,
Next time you rhyme, you'll be turned into slime!"

Harry Allan (8)
Howardian Primary School, Cardiff

The Ghost Teddy Bear

The teddy bear is as white as a marshmallow.
He doesn't like balls.
If he sees one he will freak out.
You should hide before you get tired.
He had a little glue to stick people on the wall.
He's a little tall but not too tall.
I can smell rotten eggs from the kitchen.
He can get itchy.

Rahma Mustafa Al-Qaysi (8)
Howardian Primary School, Cardiff

A Creepy Night

I woke up at 3am and I saw a sloppy, creepy, slimy monster.
I went into my bathroom and my face felt so weird,
I turned around and my room was covered in slime,
It was on my face too.
I finally got to sleep and then I heard something.
I grabbed my mum and my dog and ran.
That night was so creepy.

Lola Gent (8)
Howardian Primary School, Cardiff

The Deep Dark

I'm trying to sleep, then I'm playing hide-and-seek.
I'm staying alive
When I'm trying to hide.
Then I creep down,
What's that? Is it Tloby?
It looks blobby, well, it's yucky!
Tloby's body is outrageously slimy.
Every second, one drip slips down like sweat.

Nia Owen (8)
Howardian Primary School, Cardiff

Smooshy

Yes, I am Smooshy,
Oops, look out, I pop everywhere.
I am a monster, so I do weird stuff.
I will smoosh you up, no wonder my name is Smooshy.
I leave slime trails.
I am only alive at night.
I mean, I am good and I'm pretty nice.
Not all the time though, I can go a bit too crazy.

Charley Davis Vickers (8)
Howardian Primary School, Cardiff

Silly Something Need Something

Silly Something needs to go to the loo
Just watch out before he's about.
He lives under your bed with Ted
I think you should go to the loo.
This monster hates the poo when it's you
I need to lead my family with you
His eyes are like a bull on a bike
He is green and so mean.

Nye Brute-Woods (8)
Howardian Primary School, Cardiff

The Monster

Watch out, the Pop will send you to bed
With ice cream on your head.
He has a lion's mane
His favourite footballer is Harry Kane.
He's stinky and smelly,
He likes to watch the telly.
He'll sit by you and watch the sparks in the sky
And make you think that you can fly.

Eira Wolski (7)
Howardian Primary School, Cardiff

Untitled

As small as a slug
Jilee Jin is the scariest monster
Jilee Jin has the most legs
As colourful as a rainbow
Spikes as sharp as knives
His feet whoosh whoosh as he walks
His antennae are as black as mountains
His body is like jelly
He has a deep voice
He is very heavy.

Llywelyn Lewis (7)
Howardian Primary School, Cardiff

Marvellous Mariam

Snail is as slimy as a worm.
Wings as fluffy as cotton wool.
Skin is warty like a witch's nose.
Crash! Like a monster's feet.
Eyes like a blue sky.
Her teeth are as sharp as jagged glass.
A T-shirt as soft as the ocean.
Whoosh went the flying monster.

Mariam Amin (7)
Howardian Primary School, Cardiff

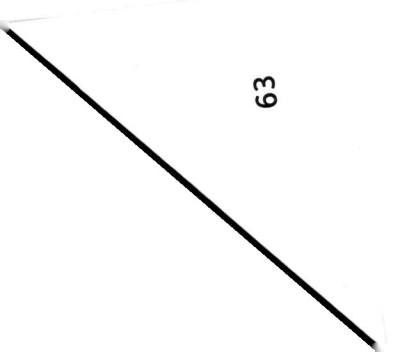

Ugly Ully

Monster as slimy as bogies.
Teeth are as smooth as a table.
As clean as a washing machine.
Smells nicer than flowers.
Eyes as bright as the sky.
Gentler than a puppy.
Ears longer than a kangaroo ear.
Trail as slimy as a snail.
Tiptoe, tiptoe!
He surprised the children.

Titi Oladebo (8)
Howardian Primary School, Cardiff

The Most Creepy And Funny Night

I saw those creepy jaws, who could it be...
The Loch Ness Monster called Loch!
Before it put its smelly hands on me
I said, "Ewww, get away from me. Oh, it's you Lochy."
Then he said, "Hi" and ran away from me,
He got my dad's eggs and ate them again.

Raya Shemshaki (8)
Howardian Primary School, Cardiff

Grinding Granny

Pitch-black eyes like a black night sky.
Most likely to chomp your head off!
Scariest of all the killers, deadly as a lion.
More deadly than Pennywise.
Skin as soft as a lions' fur.
Balloons as bumpy as a shell.
Hands as sharp as knives!
This monster is deadly.

Harlen Rochford Taylor (7)
Howardian Primary School, Cardiff

Scary Monsters

My monster creeps through the woods in the dark
Until he bumps into the bark.
Bang! Bump! Thud!
He's small and I'm tall.
His body is furry and his head.
He likes to climb onto your bed
And keep you company until you sleep.
Then a new day comes.

Rosie Thomas (7)
Howardian Primary School, Cardiff

TNT Destroyer Kills You

TNT Destroyer is lurking,
His favourite food is zombies and people.
He knows your every move
And he will kill you, so beware.
When he walks, stuff explodes!
Be careful at night and he is very dangerous
And he has powers, he can turn into any animal in the world!

Ben Davies (8)
Howardian Primary School, Cardiff

The Naughty Monster

My monster is very slimy and creepy.
Blob can sometimes be nice or mean.
Watch out because she has sprouts for breakfast.
She throws things under her bed, so her mum doesn't see.
She will hypnotise you for no reason.
Be aware, she could be lurking under your bed!

Jada Johannes (7)
Howardian Primary School, Cardiff

Praf Carp66

Praf Carp66 is as scary as a creep.
Head is as hard as a rock.
Weird as a monster.
Arms as long as wheat.
Eyes as big as a wheel.
Big as a door.
Spikes as sharp as a knife.
Brown as a tree.
Teeth as sharp as a spike.
Likes to light fires.

Lewis Walker (7)
Howardian Primary School, Cardiff

Jump Bump

He hums with a beat
But he steals your treats.
He takes your candy,
He is not handy.
He is cute but cheeky.
If you find him, he will jump on your car.
He will make a boot.
He has two boots.
He smells like candyfloss,
If you floss.

Rai Pequito (8)
Howardian Primary School, Cardiff

Amazing Amaani

Snail as slimy as a worm.
Wings as soft as a rabbit.
Skin warty like a witch's nose.
Slimy as a monster.
A monster as bumpy as a rock.
Eyes like the sky.
Teeth are as sharp as a sword.
Skin bumpy as mouldy cheese.
As deep as an ocean.

Amaani Majid (7)
Howardian Primary School, Cardiff

Spirit Rose Monster

Spirit Rose Monster is weird.
She is creepy.
People think I am evil and bad.
Spirit Rose Monster is scary,
She doesn't like a single bit of light.
You can hear scrapes on the window
And sometimes she goes under your bed to sit down by you.

Amelia Sadiq (8)
Howardian Primary School, Cardiff

The Freaky Night

One day I was walking in the freaky forest,
When I walked I saw a monster he was called Salad.
He looked like a spiky tree and a self-pen,
When you touch him that will be your end.
His favourite treats are children,
His favourite bit is the heart.

Mohamad Almezyab (8)
Howardian Primary School, Cardiff

The Head Of Steam

I was watching a movie
When I heard a terrible noise
Then I turned around and I saw a mighty monster
I'm sure it's rather freaky!
You might think, *he's not too scary!*
Well, you're wrong because he's coming for you!

Samuel Parsons (8)
Howardian Primary School, Cardiff

The Creepy Night

Ned is lying comfy in bed,
But there somewhere is a shadow of a head.
The noises that Ned can hear
Make him scared and fills him with fear.
Now he feels something as hard as a rock
And he hears the crunching bone.
Next, Ned is dead.

Angus Turton (7)
Howardian Primary School, Cardiff

Amazing Adventurous Alby

Bright red eyes like lava.
Amazing Adventures Alby is the scariest monster in the universe!
Fangs as sharp as a spear.
Poisonous skin as warty as a witch's nose.
His heavy feet go *crash! Bang!*
Wakes up bats in a cave!

Alby Atherton (7)
Howardian Primary School, Cardiff

Flexible Flora

Flexible as a piece of paper.
Nail as sharp as a knife.
A head as big as the world.
Hair is as big as a tree.
Feet as loud as ringing bells,
Waking up the sleeping children by the haunted house.
Some teeth as sharp as metal.

Flora Szabo (7)
Howardian Primary School, Cardiff

Bloodsucking Bill

Hair is as hard as a monster's roller skates.
Bloodsucking Bill is the silliest monster of all.
Teeth as soft as a nail.
Eyes as sharp as horns.
Wings are as haunted as bats!
Stomp! Stomp! went the loud monster.

Samuel Giles (7)
Howardian Primary School, Cardiff

A Beat-Box Beat

I was late for a party
Because of silly Mr Carty
But on my way
I saw the bay
I saw a breakdancer
But he was about to get a plaster
I invited him
To entertain us
And I went home
With some happy memories.

Zachary William Ait-Hammi (8)
Howardian Primary School, Cardiff

I See You

I See You's fangs will dig deep into your hands.
He will make you die and take your head.
He's a volcano ready to erupt.
He came from the basement, I was scared.
I got prepared.
He was scary, so I must be wary.

Bob McCarthy (8)
Howardian Primary School, Cardiff

Scream Monster

Monsters creeping and peeping on my ceiling.
I can smell blood, dripping down on me.
I have a feeling something is lurking with wings.
I hear claws scraping noisily.
I'm terrified, monsters are everywhere.
Beware!

Macy Thomas (8)
Howardian Primary School, Cardiff

Nightmare Bunny

My monster is as sly as a fox.
His eyesight is as round as a bird.
He has a sharp knife covered in blood,
That's as red as his enormous eyes.
He's as fluffy as a bear
But he has the mind of a maniac.

Olly Williams (7)
Howardian Primary School, Cardiff

A Creepy Crawly

There's a four-fanged monster creeping outside,
There's a four-fanged monster coming with pride,
Squashing all the trees like mushed peas.
He's coming along the road
And he wants to eat your... nose!

Akshara Madahar (8)
Howardian Primary School, Cardiff

A Slimy Night

It was on a slimy night, when my eyes were white.
He smells disgusting, like the socks I find when dusting.
Don't you dare run away because he's the best in the world
He hides under my bed, waiting to be fed.

Daniyal Ali (9)
Howardian Primary School, Cardiff

Time To Die

I am in the forest.
I am everywhere.
Be careful where you tread
Or you may end up dead!
My tail is long like a snake
And my tongue is spiky like a snake.
Watch out, you might be the next one to die!

Zachary Weston (8)
Howardian Primary School, Cardiff

My Monster

Hairy and it's scary.
It has eight eyes.
He has a big mouth
And he is really fluffy like a teddy.
You might find him under the bed.
He might find you in the morning,
He might keep you snoring.

Maja Fogarty (8)
Howardian Primary School, Cardiff

Slippery Slime

I am Slime, you'd best run
Because I will gobble you up
And if I gobble you up, I will rip you up.
I am Slime, run!
I am quick and slippery slime, run!
I am really scary with feet that smash you.

Louie Philip Smith (8)
Howardian Primary School, Cardiff

The Three-Eyed Worm Monster

My monster is hairy on its feet
And a little creepy in its eye.
My monster likes to wiggle when its feet tickle.
My monster has a horn because it's really tall
And the antenna is really tall as well.

Caia Chiu (7)
Howardian Primary School, Cardiff

Dark Wolf

He can blend in with the night
He runs like lightning and smells like garbage
He has slimy horns
He has great eyesight
He can see the whole universe
He has fangs, jagged
His name is Dark Wolf.

Abdul-Wahhab Amin (8)
Howardian Primary School, Cardiff

Slimy Siyam

As slimy as a slug.
As sticky as a sock.
As wobbly as jelly.
Its skin is pinker than the sky.
As smelly as shoes.
A black shadow monster.
He's very heavy.
As smelly as a rotten sock.

Siyam Ali (7)
Howardian Primary School, Cardiff

Beware Of Blade Blarg

I am brave.
I live in a cave.
I live here.
I have a spear
I have no fear.
Next time you go out at night,
You might want to bring a knife
Because you might be in for a fight!

Elliot Hoyt (7)
Howardian Primary School, Cardiff

Monster Suckblood

Zombie Head Legs likes to see legs.
He can hear everything.
No one could feel him because he is invisible.
Zombie Head Legs loves stealing eggs.
He smells all, even the bells.

Aleix Pacheco (8)
Howardian Primary School, Cardiff

Killer Evil Evan

Fiery eyes like a volcano erupting.
His wings are as haunting as a bat.
Killer Evil Evan, the scariest monster of all.
As slimy as a slug.
His skin smells like rotten cheese.

Evan Rhys Andrews (7)
Howardian Primary School, Cardiff

Killer Rich Slug

I am great.
I am awesome and sick.
I am really big.
With thin legs like a stick.
I have tiny eyes and six antennae
Which I use to watch you with.

Jacob William Harrison (7)
Howardian Primary School, Cardiff

Slush

He soars through the sky with a vicious scowl,
Slush flies by without a growl.
He has soft wings like an owl
And has amazing fur and the sweetest howl.

Elizabeth Stocks (7)
Howardian Primary School, Cardiff

Big Mouth Bill Monster

Hair as soft as cotton.
With eyes as red as volcanoes.
Nose as jagged as knives.
Crash! went the monster's teeth
With a purple wing.

Berguzar Masal Yalcin (7)
Howardian Primary School, Cardiff

Magnificent Monster Mia

Hair as long as Rapunzel.
Eyes as pretty as a queen.
Hair is as colourful as a rainbow.
Skin as nice as cake.
Dress as nice as every food.

Mia Cuddihy (7)
Howardian Primary School, Cardiff

Killing Adam

Fiery eyes like volcanoes
Erupting. Killing Adam,
The terrifying monster of all.
Killing Adam is as sticky as a lollipop.

Adam Zaczynski (7)
Howardian Primary School, Cardiff

The Hairy House

In a house
A hairy monster lurks
Perhaps it's searching
For a little child
In their bed
To eat it up!

Aeron William Cording (8)
Howardian Primary School, Cardiff

Shape-Shifter Monster

Hair as soft as cotton,
With eyes as red as blood.
Skin as bumpy as a rock.
Crash! went the scary monster.

Christine Zhang (7)
Howardian Primary School, Cardiff

Gravity Grabber

My name is Gravity Grabber
I use tentacles for arms and legs
I am evil
And I am super fast!

Jackson Turner (7)
Howardian Primary School, Cardiff

Oh ED Under My Bed!

This is ED under my bed,
I'm not trying to rhyme, his name really is ED!
I was scared at first, but he's okay,
We had the best time ever together!
I'll tell you one thing, and there's more...
I learnt ED's language!
Isn't that cool?
Oh, ED under my bed!
We giggled together over the pranks we did (quite a bit)!
ED is my best friend!
Remember, his name is ED,
And he's under my bed!
Oh, ED under the bed!
He jumped about, played hopscotch with me,
I swear it's not my imagination!
He likes to skip with my mum's shoelaces!
I say, "I didn't cut the laces off, I swear, I swear!"
If you don't believe me, look under *your* bed,
You'll find your own monster, yes indeed!
Oh, ED under my bed!

Naomi Pinto (8)
Millway Primary School, Duston

The Nightmare Monster

This monster only comes out at night,
because he doesn't like the daylight.
It has a mind,
but it's definitely not kind.
It will get stronger if you have nightmares, you see,
and this monster doesn't like any bee.
If the monster was to become the king,
your nightmares would come to life because of its infinity ring!
Halloween will be the scariest of them all,
anything can be haunted, even a ball.
Santa will become a zombie,
eating a fluffy onesie.
Holidays will be weird,
girls might have a beard!
The monster is oozy,
but in the day, very snoozy.
You will not want to say bye,
because a random guy will start to fly!
As you can see, having a nightmare is crazy,
so only have good dreams!

Eloise Baker (8)
Millway Primary School, Duston

The Monster!

Not all monsters turn out to be bad,
Here's one that is glad not to be bad.
Our story starts with a monster,
In the light, a beautiful monster comes to play,
But at night, a naughty beast waits to fight its prey.
But the thing is, nobody knew that she was a naughty beast,
Because they all thought she was kind and sweet!
But one day, she thought, *what about a switch?*
Maybe a personality switch, but maybe not my look.
She did as she thought and what do you know?
She turned out to be the best beast, you know!
And that goes to show,
Not all are bad!

Olivia Saunders (8)
Millway Primary School, Duston

Rhyme With Monster

Udly the monster is slow as a turtle,
But he is a wonderful bright purple!
Udly the monster is extremely short,
And he is horrible at sport.
Udly is super tricky,
But he is sticky.
He has been mean,
And he is always seen.
When he sees a worm,
He thinks that it's a germ.
When I see him, I start to panic,
Because I think that he's gigantic!
He has big feet,
And he likes to eat meat.
I was holding a toy,
And I've found out that he is a boy.

Edmund Puchovic (8)
Millway Primary School, Duston

Beware Of The Lazy Monster!

In the dark, dingy night after twilight
She roams through the street, stomping her big sloppy feet
Her big spiky horns slicing the lamp post in half
Her fierce, glowing red eyes peeping in your window
To see if you're asleep
Searching around your room like a guard.

Peaches Gooding (8)
Millway Primary School, Duston

Nightmare

There's a monster under my bed
It's big and red
It's hairy and scary
It also is probably naughty
And I don't know what to do
I woke up in the day
And there I lay
I looked under my bed
And there was nothing red
There wasn't a monster under my bed
And I was so happy
Until the clock hit noon
I went back to bed
But then I saw red again
Now my bedsheets are wet
From all the sweat
My dream was really a warning
Now the monster is planning...

Amir (10)
Real Action Butterfly School, Queens Park

Monsters In The Night

Monsters in the night
Are afraid of the light
They are so scary
Humans' vision is so blurry
Monsters live in caves
Superman comes to save
The queen monster is in charge
The king monster is really large
Monsters come in houses
Monsters eat mice
They play sneak up on people
Monsters hate sepal
So, if you ever see a monster
Do what you need to do
Turn the light on
Grab a calyx
And walk out.

Anujan Rejonald Nirubaraj (8)
Sacred Heart Primary School, Battersea

Monster Not A Reality

Is there a monster, really?
Hard to say yes or no,
But our parents do scare us,
Knowing full well there isn't any,
Let us not be fooled,
By something that doesn't exist,
Show them we are the new generation,
Come out with something new,
Old ones are outdated,
Sorry, no disrespect to old ones.

Anagha Vinod Nair (9)
Sneinton CE Primary School, Sneinton

Big Monster Eyeballs

There were big monster eyeballs, as spooky as can be.
Hanging in the haunted house and staring right at me!
I tried not to look but their eyes were red and round
Those big monster eyeballs are the creepiest in town!

Ivie Daniella Enoma (8)
Sneinton CE Primary School, Sneinton

Sensitive Monsters Come!

R inging is not what she likes in bed
O ranges are her favourite fruits
S ongs are her favourite hobbies
E ggs are her favourite food for dinner
B unnies are her favourite things
U nicorns are her favourite fake things
D inosaurs she sees, there are four boys but they are actually girls and boys.

Ebony Setter (6)
Sowerby Village CE (VC) Primary School, Sowerby Bridge

Watch Out!

M ars
A ngry when he is sad
R ed eyes
S miley face
H ates photos
M ean face
A ll enormous
L ittle
L umpy legs
O range legs
W icked fire blasters.

M assive ghost
A ngry dreams
N o nose.

James William Speight (6)
Sowerby Village CE (VC) Primary School, Sowerby Bridge

Mattster The Mean Monster

M ad face
A pple-shaped eyes
T iny tentacles
T ypical head
S limy hair
T omato nose
E gg yolk splatted over him
R obotic arms.

JJ Riley (6)
Sowerby Village CE (VC) Primary School, Sowerby Bridge

The Sticky Man

S ticky eyes
L urky and silly thoughts
I ncredible blobs of slime shoot out of his head
M assive head blows up
Y ou fall from the end of his fingers.

Zachary Pukl (6)
Sowerby Village CE (VC) Primary School, Sowerby Bridge

Marshy Saves The Day

M arsh food that he likes
A nd he likes normal food as well
R obot fish he likes
S nores
H e eats lots of stuff
Y um yum, people to eat.

Ryan Martin Lynch (6)
Sowerby Village CE (VC) Primary School, Sowerby Bridge

Pinkey Comes And Scares

P inkey body
I ncredible tricks
N ever comes out, he's scared
K ind monster
E gg head
Y ellow stripes.

Libby Lewis (7)
Sowerby Village CE (VC) Primary School, Sowerby Bridge

Watch Out For The Claw

M onster claws
R oars loudly

C lumsy
L ight orange eyes
A rms are long
W eird wings.

Amelia Pollard (6)
Sowerby Village CE (VC) Primary School, Sowerby Bridge

Scary Monster

S ix legs
C lumsy
A nnoying
R aging
Y ellow body.

Milli-Sue Graham (6)
Sowerby Village CE (VC) Primary School, Sowerby Bridge

Dave's First Day At School

Today is Dave's first day at school,
He hopes the other monsters think he's cool
Dave is feeling nervous today,
Because things don't always go his way
He loves to run in lots of races,
But Dave is so clumsy, he trips over his laces
Dave is amazing at monster art,
But crazy Dave knocks over the paint cart
His picture is ruined and he feels sad,
Everything he is doing turns out bad
All the other monsters think Dave is silly,
Apart from his best friend, Lily
Come on, Dave, keep on going,
It doesn't matter if you are clumsy or crazy or silly
Because, to me, you are the perfect friend,
You are funny and caring and kind.

Evie Williams (7)
St Mark's CE (VA) Primary School, Talbot Village

Citsalp The Monster

Citsalp jumped abruptly out of bed
He lived in the deep dark wood in a shed
He sucked up all of the sun's rays...
15,000,000 degrees stored in his tummy for lots of days
Black and towering, his huge shadow emerged
Sparks exploded, enormous flames, Citsalp submerged
Through the smoke, his orange, fiery eyes
Glared around the world hungrily, under all the skies
His four arms stretched out, searching for plastic
His ambition was, once again, to 'make the world fantastic'
Citsalp scoured cities, towns, hospitals and factories
Rubbish dumps, shops, rivers, lakes and seas!
His levers thudded, clattering sounds echoed
Cogs inside him churned and bellowed
Jagged cracks appeared in the ground
Citsalp munched all the plastic that could be found

Citsalp's eyes blared orange, his tummy gurgled with glee
At last, he had rid the world of plastic and set it free!

Ryan Hegan (9)
St Mark's CE (VA) Primary School, Talbot Village

The Red Fantasy

He roams at night and roars in light
His horns furrow into enormous fright
His rising tentacles and gigantic grin
Is enough to fit us all in
His flaming eyes and terrible lies
Tie up the night with beauty's twilight skies
His deafening stamps and mighty strength
Is so much more than all his length
His sticky pads and major spot
Is enough to make us all report
His rickety smell and large flowing eyes
Are all you need to stay alive
His hunger to eat is children's naughty feet
It's also Red Fantasy's favourite treat
A wrinkling nose to sniff with
A magical myth to live with
And a cheeky grin to pin with
Red Fantasy stays under your bed
While you drift off into your head
So stay still and close your weary eyes
And count your leaping sheep

'Cause if you open your eyes
You'll be startled by a terrible surprise!

Emma Gheorghe (9)
St Mark's CE (VA) Primary School, Talbot Village

Toby, My Wardrobe Monster

A monster lives in my wardrobe, he is very shy
He wears shorts, a shirt and a silver tie
He loves to make slime when it is school time
He makes an awful mess that I have to clean up
But as soon as I get home, the wardrobe doors shut
I know he's in there because he snores like a pig
I would love to see him but he is always hidden
His small teeth and rainbow-coloured hair
To be fair, he looks very scared
As white as a ghost
So I make him beans on toast
He says, "It's the yummiest thing I've ever tasted in my life,"
It is getting late, so I tuck him into my bed
As I walk to the door, I hear Toby snore...

Lexi Mae Shakespeare (8)
St Mark's CE (VA) Primary School, Talbot Village

A Monster Misunderstood!

Exploring the forest at first light,
I had the most awful fright!
Two giant tree hands suddenly did appear,
Filling my heart up with fear.
I tried to wiggle and get past,
But the giant had me in his grasp.
Root-like feet and skin as bark,
And on his face a nasty mark.
In a soft and gentle voice, he spoke,
And warned me of the horrid folk,
Who lived in the village nearby,
And cut forest trees day and night.
The monster would scare them when he could,
For he didn't like them stealing wood.
I promised I'd help him as much as I could,
For he was a monster misunderstood.

Sa'ad Rehan Sami (8)
St Mark's CE (VA) Primary School, Talbot Village

Tilly Ned

Can I introduce my monster
Her name is Tilly Ned
She has wings and high-heeled shoes
And a tiara on her head.

She's different to most monsters
She doesn't like to scare
The important thing to Tilly Ned
Is what she's going to wear.

She's friendly and she's cute,
She's fluffy and she's kind
She's colourful and happy
With nice thoughts on her mind.

I wish that you could meet her
She's my very special friend
But you can't because she's invisible
To all but me, the end.

Josie Aston (7)
St Mark's CE (VA) Primary School, Talbot Village

Green-Tongued Crud

Screeching fangs as he eats his appalling food every now and then,
His smelly, hairy armpits smelling like revolting sick,
And baby sick mixed and boiled with someone else's sweaty, cheesy socks,
Soaring through the sky and then vomiting onto your head
Total Crud sickness,
The worst sickness you can get in your big mouth
Makes you clean his big bottom with your lovely clean hands,
About to turn your hands more pungent and smelly,
Makes you soothe his infected verrucas with a hair from a used toothbrush.

Christopher Ngwenya Pickering (8)
St Mark's CE (VA) Primary School, Talbot Village

Help, There's A Monster!

Blood is dripping down his face,
Monster maniac is on the chase

Stomping through the stormy night,
Watch out for his venomous bite!

See his glowing purple eyes,
Hear him telling vicious lies

Touch his scaly, brown and green skin,
Smell his breath, it's worse than a bin

Green gunge is oozing out of his ears,
And the warts on his nose make you tremble with fear

Get under your bed covers and scream,
Over there, he's planning his horrid scheme.

Elsy Beales (9)
St Mark's CE (VA) Primary School, Talbot Village

The Maths Monster Method

The Maths Monster snuck closer as darkness fell
He crept along the path, hoping nobody could tell
Then it climbed the house and took a rest
He looked inside and saw a child snuggled in a nest
He jumped through the window and landed with a crash
The child woke up, starting to make a dash
But then the monster blocked the door
Then the child could not wait much more
The monster leapt and gobbled the child
And this was when the monster would get more wild.

Jayden You (7)
St Mark's CE (VA) Primary School, Talbot Village

Where To Find Cheeky Chops?

Hiding in a basement, watch out below!
Hiding in a house, oh no, that is a mouse
Hiding in a tree, nope, that's just a bee
Hiding in a bed, oh no, that's just a sleepy head
Where oh where could Cheeky Chops be?
He is not in a basement or in a house
He is not hiding in a tree or a bed
So where is he? *Plop!*
There he is, hopping around me,
He was hiding in the bin
I wonder if he thought he would win!

Felicity Tschoepe (8)
St Mark's CE (VA) Primary School, Talbot Village

Monsters, Monsters, Watch Out, Monsters

Monsters are secretive, scary, hiding
Looking to eat whatever they see
Hunting monsters are coming to town
So be careful, watch out for monsters
They are soon going to get you
And if you are wondering where the monsters are hiding,
They hide everywhere
Because small ones can hide in very small places,
So they might be right behind you
Watch out, carefully, so they don't eat you
Beware of monsters.

Mirabella Twardowska (7)
St Mark's CE (VA) Primary School, Talbot Village

Slobberball The Vandal

Slobberball is gross,
He loves to roast
And eats the most
He will scare the cats
And eat the rats
And he will slobber all over
Your beautiful mats!
He breaks into your house
And he will break your pots
He looks like a pile of big, fat dots
He would stay up in the night
And would love a fight
His name is Slobberball
The gruesome monster
Come back soon, tomorrow noon.

Josh Horgan (9)
St Mark's CE (VA) Primary School, Talbot Village

Monsters In Town

These are monsters, very crazy indeed
Very fun every day, playing in town
Thinking of monsters secretly
See them roaring very loudly
Every person suspicious about them
Not knowing if they are real
Wait, things will never work
You never know where monsters are in this world
Hide, they are coming,
Seek them, if you dare
They are everywhere...
Monsters, monsters, everywhere!

Ava-Louise Parris (7)
St Mark's CE (VA) Primary School, Talbot Village

The Fluffy Monster

In the deep, dark jungles,
As tall as a tree
The fluffy monster lives peacefully

Fluffy has two small eyes,
The colour of fire
His hair is like TV wires

He has a brilliant blue tongue,
His fur is purple and green
He can always be seen!

He likes to chew on dead slugs!
The funniest thing of all
He sleeps with a cuddly teddy and his ball!

Annabel Hitchins (8)
St Mark's CE (VA) Primary School, Talbot Village

Monsters, Monsters, Mythical Monsters

M agical, mythical, monstrous monsters
O bnoxious, odious, outrageous monsters
N aughty, nasty, noisy monsters
S melly, scowling, shape-shifting monsters
T errific, terrifying, tough monsters
E normous, energetic, extraordinary monsters
R evolting, repulsive, ridiculous monsters

Monsters, monsters, mythical monsters.

Sam Treliving (7)
St Mark's CE (VA) Primary School, Talbot Village

Scampier Needed The Loo

One day in a storm
A monster with horns
Was eating a rock
When he heard a knock.
So he went to the door
But fell on the floor
And dropped his rock
On his sock.
He didn't know what to do
Then he needed a poo
So he picked up the rock
And threw away the sock.
But he still needed to do
What he had to do
So he ran to the loo.

Tasmin Addis (9)
St Mark's CE (VA) Primary School, Talbot Village

Caliban: A Crazy Creature

C lever Caliban can control anything on the island
A wful cape, that's what Caliban has
L ong teeth, he can bite anything
I ntelligent and sneaky, he likes to play tricks
B orn to the king of the island
A bsurdly, Caliban is half-fish and half-bear
N ever make Caliban cross, otherwise he'll attack.

Louis Paull (7)
St Mark's CE (VA) Primary School, Talbot Village

The Curry Monster

This is Bobby,
Bobby is green
Bobby is funny,
Bobby isn't mean

I saw him last night,
He is very nice
He loves spicy food but it gave him a fright,
When he was eating curry with a hot spice

Bobby is magical,
Bobby is mystical
He is amazing
And he is my best friend
Our friendship will never end.

Zara Guppy (9)
St Mark's CE (VA) Primary School, Talbot Village

Help! Monsters Are Everywhere!

Pebbles was a cheeky monster.
Who came from Planet Bluster.
One day, he crashed down to Earth.
He ended up in my lounge, holding a teddy, asking its worth.
He asked to stay in my house, and promised to be good.
He hummed and hawed then said he would.
Now I have a best friend called Pebbles
And he is a naughty little rebel.

Summer-Bella Hack (7)
St Mark's CE (VA) Primary School, Talbot Village

A Monster Under My Bed

A monster lives under my bed
But he's not scary so I call him Fred
His texture is slimy
But he's also very grimy
So now you know what he's like
You might consider calling him Mike.

George William Lowton (7)
St Mark's CE (VA) Primary School, Talbot Village

Monsters

Monsters, monsters, monsters
Gruesome, some slimy monsters
Hidden in the dark
So only come out if you dare
Monsters, monsters, monsters.

Josh Jabulani Nyathi (7)
St Mark's CE (VA) Primary School, Talbot Village

Dragons

Dragons, dragons, dragons
Huge, mighty, scaly dragons
Hungry, fierce, fire-breathing dragons
Dragons, dragons, dragons.

Layla Kwok (7)
St Mark's CE (VA) Primary School, Talbot Village

The Scary Snorgon

I was sitting alone at midnight when
I heard a screech
Like a mouse having a fright!
It was a monster!
But it did not harm me.
Instead, it made my house a big, big wreck!
I was very mad!
It had an odd nose
That looked like a rose.
I told the monster to leave
But he said in a squeaky voice,
"Not till you give me some cheese!"
So I gave him some cheese
And he left in a flash
And ever since then, he's not been seen.

Darcy Joseph Fletcher (8)
The Compass Primary Academy, Kettering

Cuddles The Monster

Cuddles likes to cuddle people
And he will go and knock on people's doors to get a cuddle from children.
As he goes around for cuddles, people always ask what his favourite thing to do is
And people always ask what his favourite food is!
He says, "Marshmallows!"
And they say he's cute.
He's as cuddly as a little kid
And as fluffy as a teddy bear.
The children who cuddle him
Always say they hear a squeeze noise and a tiny scream.

Bethany Hull (8)
The Compass Primary Academy, Kettering

Super Snugglebum

Snuggelbum is a big green monster,
He is always hungry and angry, so it makes him hangry.

Snugglebum has a fridge in his stomach so he can eat,
He's as green as grass (it's gross!).

Snugglebum's slime is super squeaky,
His face is always messy with food.

His curly hair goes all over the place when he eats,
He's the complete opposite of pretty.

He loves everything,
From broccoli to Hershey's!

Maria Ignat (9)
The Compass Primary Academy, Kettering

Shifty's Secret

This is Shifty!
I have to tell you a secret...
She pretends to be good in the day,
But at night...
She steals most of the food at the Monster Mart!
Grumble! Growl!
The monsters are as hungry as the Minotaur!
If you find her stealing,
Squeal!
She will threaten you if you call the Creature Savers!

Sanjeda Ahmed (8)
The Compass Primary Academy, Kettering

Eye Brawl

I have a pet monster,
I call him Eye Brawl.

My sister has a monster,
But you don't want to meet that!

It's as creepy as the Gruffalo,
I was so scared, I felt like it was watching me!

I felt like running, I was so scared,
Oh! But Eye Brawl was there!

Harrison Bridgman (9)
The Compass Primary Academy, Kettering

It's About Friendly Monster Called Samly

The friendly red spotty monster called Samly
He stomps like a giant
But he is friendly like a puppy.
He does not like mean monsters or people!

"Yes, Harmonaii is right!
I am friendly
And my favourite colour is red.
Can you please be my friend?"

Harmonaii Lily Jean Wood (8)
The Compass Primary Academy, Kettering

Eerie Monster

He scares like thunder rumbling.
He likes to eat a lot.
Sometimes he will eat humans.
Would you like to be his friend?
Can you survive the tower?
Can you catch it?
Could you be lucky enough?
His claws are as sharp as wolf claws!
It will slice you!

Wiktor Kopania (8)
The Compass Primary Academy, Kettering

Blue Bluey

Bluey is a furry monster
He is very friendly as a pet
He is awake at night and asleep all day
He wants more care, that's all he wants to get
You will want to see his fur
I really like him
Just listen to him purr
Do you want to be his friend?

Aiden Knell (8)
The Compass Primary Academy, Kettering

Goodfluffy

I found a monster under my bed
He's a fluffy shape-shifter who is good
His antennae eyes can see 100 miles away
He is as fluffy as a fluffy teddy bear
His footsteps sound like a rumble from a volcano
Then he went to sleep.

Thomas Pickford (8)
The Compass Primary Academy, Kettering

Yellow Cake

This is Yellow Cake.
She loves eating cakes, yellow food.
She has a curly body, dangerous horns.
She has a long, spotty tongue.
She is as hungry as a bear!
Her back is as fluffy as a lion.
Her tummy is rumbling loud...

Zara Treadwell (8)
The Compass Primary Academy, Kettering

Red Head Is On Fire!

Red Head has deadly horns,
He is as scary as the Gruffalo,
With feet as sharp as thorns,
Red Head is one of the biggest shape-shifters in his family,
He's as spiky as a dinosaur.
With a big loud *roar!*

Jaidan Webb (7)
The Compass Primary Academy, Kettering

Beastly Life

He comes out at night
ready to fight!

He eats children for a treat
and can't be beaten!

His fangs are as red as blood
and he lives in the mud!

He goes *tiptoe, tiptoe.*

Zack Lewis Whiteman (8)
The Compass Primary Academy, Kettering

Scorry

He has a scaly body,
He has scary, white eyes,
With little pink antlers.
He loves eating fingers,
He is as scaly as a snake,
He has giant eyes like a tiger!
He went *splosh!* in a goopy pool.

Maisie Bell (7)
The Compass Primary Academy, Kettering

Bunnychain

This is Bunnychain.
Bunnychain has a powerful protective star-heart.
Bunnychain has scared over 10,000 little kids!
Bunnychain was so hungry that he bought 10,000 burgers
He screamed, "Yummy!"

Devon Cook (8)
The Compass Primary Academy, Kettering

Bruno

There is a monster as big as a gorilla,
As purple as purple paint,
And as evil as a crocodile.

His name is Bruno,
And he smashes plates!
Smash!

He's always hungry.

Cameron Rhys Wonfor (8)
The Compass Primary Academy, Kettering

Pink Marble The Vampire

Marble loves drinking blood,
She looks cute on the outside and deadly on the inside,
Marble is as pink as a rose,
And the reason she is called Marble,
Is because her eyes are like big blue marbles!

Abby Chamberlain (8)
The Compass Primary Academy, Kettering

Mr Stink

Mr Stink is a giant monster and he stomps so loud!
Mr Stink is very scary because he has a lot of spikes on him!
Mr Stink is very fluffy because he has fluffy hair.
He is as hungry as a shark and lion!

Faith Lillie Elrick (7)
The Compass Primary Academy, Kettering

Spooky Monster

He is annoying and green with a wicked sense of humour.
He has a pointy and spiky tail on his back.
His teeth are sharp and bumpy like a dinosaur's.
His eyes are bright and glimmery on his face.

Ashley Ridley (10)
The Compass Primary Academy, Kettering

Yellow Apollo

My yellow Apollo
He is hairy
And he is as fat as a table!
He eats lots of food and bananas and lemons and slime.
He sleeps at one in the morning
And wakes up at twelve in the afternoon!

Yaw Boateng Amoakohene (8)
The Compass Primary Academy, Kettering

Rose

Rose is always pretty,
She always wears a bow,
And she puts them in a row,
She's always kind to others,
She's as pink as a pig.
Bang! She slammed the door.

Emily Collett (8)
The Compass Primary Academy, Kettering

Fluffy

The fluffy, spotty, kind monster came to tea,
His fur ran down his tail on his pink body.
He was as fluffy as a hamster,
His fur was blowing in the wind,
Woo! Woo! Woo!

Maisey Angela Horrigan (7)
The Compass Primary Academy, Kettering

Roller

Roller is colossal so he can smash buildings!
Roller is spiky so he can kill his enemies!
Roller is kind so he doesn't kill friends.
Roller is as spiky as a hedgehog.

Dexter Whitney-Green (7)
The Compass Primary Academy, Kettering

Goke

He has fangs as sharp as a sword.
His eyes are as big as a human.
His horns are as long as a giraffe's neck.
He chews as loud as an elephant.
Crunch!

Harley Chiam (9)
The Compass Primary Academy, Kettering

Sally

The tall monster will give you a scare,
But Sally is friendly!
His spiky tail is purple and blue,
He's as spotty as a leopard,
And he roars like thunder!

Scarlett Rayner (9)
The Compass Primary Academy, Kettering

Puff The Monster

Puff is a cute dragon,
He has a green, spiky tail.
Puff is as green as grass,
Puff is as small as a dog.
Puff yawns like a tiger,
Rrrrr!

Violet Serendipity Haywood (9)
The Compass Primary Academy, Kettering

The Story Of Disgusting

His body is as spiky as a hedgehog,
His spikes are as gooey as a dinosaur,
His blue hairs are as long as a hedgehog's spikes,
He is as slimy as vomit.

Kaja Kajszczarek (7)
The Compass Primary Academy, Kettering

My Monster

His long legs will stompy you,
He has one eye and he will see you when you sleep,
He can turn into different shapes,
He is intelligent like a scientist.

Ivo Otocki (7)
The Compass Primary Academy, Kettering

My Fluffy Monster

She is a tall, loud, fluffy monster,
She is a great, huge, awesome monster.
She is as red as a strawberry,
Her body is fluffy enough to lie on!

Ellie-Louise Frost (9)
The Compass Primary Academy, Kettering

Mr Spike

Mr Spike has spikes on his head and his body.
Mr Spike is red and hard.
Mr Spike has four big eyes.
Mr Spike is as spiky as a stinging nettle.

Thomas Angusdon Rogers (7)
The Compass Primary Academy, Kettering

Spotty

The spotty, hairy monster's name is Spotty.
Spotty likes lots of food!
He is as hairy as a lion's mane,
His hair swishes side to side.

Isabella Cross (8)
The Compass Primary Academy, Kettering

Scary Monster

My monster is scary,
This monster is hairy!
This is a mad monster,
Hungry as a shark!
My monster bangs and stomps the floor hard!

Hollie-Beth Howlin (7)
The Compass Primary Academy, Kettering

Basilisk

Its giant scales run down its back.
It is as green as a mossy rock.
The Basilisk chomps on the bear.
It is larger than a building.

Carmelo Chowanski (9)
The Compass Primary Academy, Kettering

Cuddly Monster

Kind as a friend
Lovely as a dress, pink and purple
As beautiful as everything in the world
Cuddly in the school.

Reese Stapleford (9)
The Compass Primary Academy, Kettering

My Scary Monster

My monster has horns on its red body.
My monster has sharp fangs.
He is faster than a cheetah!
Bang!

Archie Roe (7)
The Compass Primary Academy, Kettering

Mr Mike

It has big fangs.
It is very hairy.
It is very, very scary.
My monster looks like a giant!

Blake Sidney Robert Smith-Edwards (7)
The Compass Primary Academy, Kettering

Kipper

He is a small and short monster,
He is as small as a mouse!
He has a big mouth like a T-rex!

Harri Taylor (9)
The Compass Primary Academy, Kettering

Big, Bad, Brutal Barny

Once you start reading this,
You're under his spell,
His hair is like a flame swaying in the wind,
His beady eyes are watching from Hell,
He is as sneaky as a snake after his prey,
Bang! Bang! His feet stomped and everything around him fell,
Watch out! The horrible beast is here,
But no one knows,
The second you see him, there's no going back,
Once you finish reading this,
You'd better watch your back!

Michael Wetton (10)
Ysgol Pum Heol, Llanelli

Hairy To Scary

My monster is called Hairy,
He isn't really scary,
He's scared of under his bed
And makes me go all red,
Sometimes, I feel sad,
Then Hairy feels all bad,
But, now I've realised,
I can't look at Hairy's eyes,
He was called Hairy,
But, now, he's called Scary,
He hides under your bed,
Get your parents to check,
But, don't be scared,
Just don't look behind you!

Cadi Fflur Desouza (10)
Ysgol Pum Heol, Llanelli

YOUNG WRITERS INFORMATION

We hope you have enjoyed reading this book – and that you will continue to in the coming years.

If you're a young writer who enjoys reading and creative writing, or the parent of an enthusiastic poet or story writer, do visit our website **www.youngwriters.co.uk**. Here you will find free competitions, workshops and games, as well as recommended reads, a poetry glossary and our blog. There's lots to keep budding writers motivated to write!

If you would like to order further copies of this book, or any of our other titles, then please give us a call or order via your online account.

Young Writers
Remus House
Coltsfoot Drive
Peterborough
PE2 9BF
(01733) 890066
info@youngwriters.co.uk

Join in the conversation!
Tips, news, giveaways and much more!

f YoungWritersUK   **🐦** @YoungWritersCW